I Feel Too Much:

A How-To Guide For The Beginner Empath

Alicia McBride, RYT, RMT

As You Wish Publishing, LLC
Connect@asyouwishpublishing.com
www.asyouwishpublishing.com

ISBN-13: 978-1-951131-04-3

Library of Congress Control Number: 2020910133

Edited by Todd Schaefer

Printed in the United States of America.

Nothing in this book or any affiliations with this book is a substitute for medical or psychological help. If you are needing help please seek it.

For my babies Aiden and Riley.

"The answers you seek are already
inside of you."

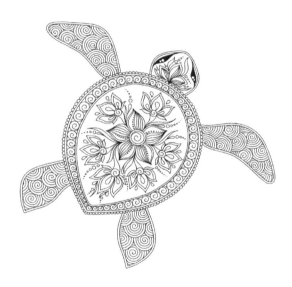

Table of Contents

Introduction

Hi there!

Welcome to the next level of your life! You already have the knowledge and the power. Use this guide book as a tool to help you reach down and find it. Your healing and your path are completely in your hands and in your heart. How you use these tools and how you transform your life is up to you. Remember to be kind and gentle to yourself throughout your journey here. Life is a work in progress. Sometimes you'll read the whole book, go through all the steps, and find you're doing really well, but then the shit hits the fan, and you need to regroup. Pick up the book again, re-read the step that you need the most, and go for it. I truly hope it helps you to find yourself, find your best life path, heal your soul, and let your light shine bright.

With Love & Gratitude,

Alicia McBride

My Story: The Baggage

If you are an empath, you are sensitive to the invisible energy that surrounds all things on earth. Everything is made up of energy, and you can feel it. You have the ability to feel the emotions and energy of those around you. This can include people, animals, plants, and energy from objects. Empaths can easily absorb the energy of others and take it on as their own (in the beginning, this happens without you even knowing it). If someone is sad, you feel their sadness, if someone is having physical pain, you may feel their pain, physically, in your body. You may not realize it's happening.

For the majority of my life, I absorbed the energy of everyone around me. I had no idea it was happening; I had no idea that it wasn't mine. When I was little, I was the friend that my friends came to with their troubles, I could always make them feel better. I didn't know it was because, in addition to allowing them to vent their problems, I was taking on their pain. They felt better, and I kept it as mine. As I grew up, adults came to me with their problems, and I talked with them and took their pain away, and kept it as my own.

When I was a senior in high school, I wanted to be a guidance counselor, and I have a Bachelor's degree in psychology because I wanted to help people. The more people I "helped," the more pain I took on. You can see where this is going. This was incredibly unhealthy behavior for them and me. Taking someone's pain away is great, temporarily. Still, everyone has their own path, and everyone needs to work through their own troubles. It's better to empower someone to help themselves, not to be a quick pain release. (Nothing against a quick pain release, sometimes you need that to help you get through the moment, but then you need to work on the deeper issue.) During my first four years in college, I decided psychology wasn't for me, and I went on to get an Associate's degree in interior design.

During this period in my life is when shit hit the fan. I was in my early 20's and had carried and added on 20 some years of other people's baggage. I was depressed, suicidal, and I didn't know why. I took medication, but it was a temporary Band-Aid, and I needed to get to the root cause. At first, I went the traditional direction with medicine and therapy. It didn't work. I was still carrying the weight of the world in my body. I felt heavy, I was beyond tired and exhausted, I was overwhelmed—everything was too big. No amount of quiet time was enough. I didn't know what I needed. I was a wreck.

I eventually found alternative healing therapies: Yoga, Acupuncture, Massage, and Reiki. I didn't know how they worked, but I trusted the effects that I was feeling. During my first Reiki treatment, the practitioner told me that I carried a lot of other people's energies with me, and she cleared them. She didn't use the word Empath, and I didn't think anything of it. It was my first experience, and I didn't know what to expect. I kept doing these alternative therapies, I became a Yoga Instructor (I still love teaching!), and I had Acupuncture and Massage regularly. I started to feel better.

Then, in my mid 30's, I read an article about Empaths. It completely rocked my world; it totally changed my life (for the better). I finally understood it. I understood what was happening to me all those years. I understood where the depression came from. I didn't know what to do about it, but just *knowing* what I am and what was going on was a great relief. I fumbled my way through. I read everything I could find on Empaths and related topics. I didn't talk to anyone close to me about this. I thought they would think that I was crazy, so I went online and found groups of so many other people, just like me.

Many other people who have gone through what I went through and who shared my experiences and fears were there for me, and they didn't think I was crazy. It was beautiful. Fast forward, and here I am on the other side of that journey. I am no longer depressed. I am empowered. I am "out" with my abilities, and I feel the best when I am my true, authentic self. I can no longer hide, and I will no longer carry the weight of everyone else's baggage. I will show you how I did it and what worked for me. I want to empower you and help you through your journey. Take my hand. I will hold it with love and light and help you to heal yourself. You can do it.

STEP

One

Ground & Protect

Step 1
Ground & Protect

The very first step to helping yourself heal is to ground and protect. What does that mean? You are probably carrying around loads of other people's emotions, baggage, and physical pains, along with many years of your own trauma, baggage, and emotions. All of that is mixed together and piled on top of you. It's heavy, and it's dragging you down.

How did it get there? Let's talk about auras and energy fields. Everyone is made up of energy and radiates a low level of electricity called an electromagnetic field. There is so much information out there about auras and what people perceive. People believe there are different layers of your aura, and each layer corresponds to a different state of health. Each layer is represented by a different color. There are many books and articles with information about aura colors and what they represent. Lots of people have different opinions about how many layers there are and what they represent. We are not going to get into all of that here.

But I'll give you my two cents. I believe that auras and the electromagnetic energy field that we all emit are one and the same. Think of the bigger picture. Nothing is separate; we are all connected. We are all the same but have differences that make us unique, and everyone is special. Everyone has different strengths and weaknesses that make us all special, and yet we all have things in common that make us all the same. We are all connected. We all emit electricity from our bodies, and we can feel it, and sometimes we can see it. You can give it whatever name you want, it's the same energy. For our purposes, I'm going to call it an energy field.

Can you feel other people's energy fields? Absolutely. This is the reason that you are here, reading this book. You can feel other people's energy, and you can take it on as your own. You can project your energy onto other people. You can take energy from someone else. You can manipulate energy. It might be scary. It might be totally unbelievable. You don't have to believe a word that I am saying, but something inside of you might know that it's true. You, my friend, are powerful.

Can you see other people's energy fields? For some, seeing energy fields is second nature and comes easily, and for others, it takes practice. I started seeing energy fields by accident, of course. I didn't know what the glow was, so I ignored it. Then one day, I was staring at myself in the mirror, and I thought, "Oh my God, that's my aura!" It was very close to my skin, a mixture of yellow and green light, and it was moving over my shoulder. It was very cool to see. Then things got a little easier, and I started seeing other people's energy fields, also by accident. They would just appear as I was talking to them. Then, I could connect with people's energy through distance. I could see their energy field even though I had never met them in person and had no idea what they looked like, physically. I could see and feel their energy.

I have seen energy fields that are very close to the skin. I have seen some that are a few inches away from the body. I have also seen very large fields so brilliant and so beautiful. It was an amazing experience. Some are quiet, and some are very loud. They are always moving, and I have always seen colors. For me, the most common colors that I have seen are white and yellow, but I have also seen green, purple, violet, deep red, and a range of blues.

Are there different layers? Do all the colors have different meanings? It's very likely. With all of the information out there, I know what I feel, I know what I see, and sometimes I just know. I'm sharing all of this with you because I know you can too. Give it whatever name you want, fill in whatever details that work best with what you believe, and know, you can feel it.

The first thing we need to do is get you to stop taking on someone else's energy and keeping it as yours. You don't need to carry the weight of the world. You can carry your own baggage and give the rest back. Grounding and protecting is a visualization technique that will allow you to release the energy that isn't yours and protect you from collecting more. Let's try it.

Start by sitting or lying in a relaxed position. Let go of your expectations of what meditation looks and feels like, and do what feels right for you. Close your eyes and take a few slow, deep breaths. I'll wait, go ahead. When you are ready, begin to imagine roots coming out of your feet, traveling through the ground, down into the earth, and wrapping around the earth's core. Feel the warmth of the center of the earth. See the fiery colors swirling. Feel rooted, and securely connected to the earth and the ground. Be at peace, knowing you are safe and secure; you are supported by nature and the earth. You are loved. Close your eyes again and take a few more slow, deep breaths. Be here. Stay here for as long as you need.

Imagine a brilliant white or golden light coming from the center of the Earth. It is traveling up the roots, up through your feet, up your legs and your torso. It travels down your arms and up over your shoulders, neck, and head. Feel the warmth. See the light surrounding you. See it surrounding your entire body, flowing over your skin, all around you, and up and over your head. Feel beautiful. See yourself completely engulfed in this beautiful bright white and golden light. Smile and feel its warmth. Feel safe and happy. Breathe here a few breaths.

See the light moving away from your skin, about a foot away from your body. See it becoming more solid but still flexible, an oval-shape surrounding your body, a shield to protect you from outside energy. Feel the safety inside of your shield. Know with your whole being that you are protected, you are safe. Close your eyes, and feel your energy, feel your power, feel the shield. Breathe a few slow, deep breaths. You are safe. You are loved. The universe loves and supports you on your path.

Take a release breath. Inhale through your nose and open your mouth to release. Take two more if you need to. Come back to your center. Feel refreshed. Smile. You are beautiful. You are an awesome person. You are loved.

This is a longer visualization. Try doing this when you feel heavy, run-down, or overwhelmed. You can also practice a shorter version and make it quick when you need a fast pick me up or when you need to prepare for an intense situation. If you are headed into the grocery store, to a party, or to the office, and you know you will be bombarded with energy, quickly see the roots. Feel grounded, and visualize the light shield surrounding you.

You can do this as often as necessary. It's especially important in the beginning to do it frequently as a reminder that you don't want other people's energy sticking to you. I have a similar "Ground and Protect" meditation and visualization up on YouTube, you can find it here: https://youtu.be/x2OC11KZwG4.

Meditation is just one way to ground yourself. Some additional ideas to help with grounding are crystals, cleansing baths, covering your crown, focusing on your breath, mountain pose, tuning forks, binaural beats, and earthing.

Crystals: There are so many types of crystals, and information about crystals is a book on its own. Crystals used for grounding are Hematite, Smoky Quartz, Black Tourmaline, Apache Tear, Jade, Jet, Agate, Obsidian, Tiger's eye, and Jasper. Crystals are wonderful. You can sit them all over your house, sleep with them under your pillow, stick them in your purse or wallet, or in your pocket. You can hold them and rub them as a reminder or use them kind of like a fidget spinner. They are so helpful.

Cleansing Baths: Take a nice warm bath with Epsom salt, Sea salt, Himalayan salt, or a mixture of all three. You can use essential oils like Ylang Ylang, lavender, spruce, rosewood, frankincense, or sandalwood. Soak for as long as you want, take slow deep breaths, and ease your mind.

Cover your Crown: I know this sounds funny, but I do it all the time, and it works. Energy (and heat) is released from the top of your head, and the bottom of your feet. To keep the energy inside of your space, cover the top of your head. It works best if the bottoms of your feet are also touching the floor or another surface. You can stand or sit with your feet flat on a surface, and put your hands on the top of your head. Breathe here for a couple of minutes, and if you can, close your eyes. I also like to use a heating pad because I get cold so easily. I sit on the couch with my feet flat, and a heating pad on my head. No joke, it's fantastic. I had even used a sweatshirt when I didn't have a heating pad. If you write a post asking for it on my Facebook wall, I might share a photo!

Focus on your Breath: You can do this almost anytime and anywhere (please be safe). This also helps reduce anxiety. If you get dizzy or light-headed, please stop and breathe normally. Start by taking slow deep breaths. Inhale and exhale through your nose. Pay attention to your breathing. Feel your belly rise and fall with each long inhale and complete exhale. Feel your breath inside of your body. If you want, you can take some release breaths, inhale fully through your nose then open your mouth to exhale. Continue taking long deep breaths, inhale and exhale through your nose. If you can safely close your eyes, do so. Pay attention to your breath. When you are ready, open your eyes and breathe normally.

Mountain Pose: I love yoga! Stand up tall with your feet firmly planted on the floor at hip-width distance. Bend your knees ever so slightly. Tuck in your tail bone. Squeeze in your pelvic floor muscles (the Kegel muscles, the ones that stop you from peeing). Squeeze in your belly muscles. Press your heart forward and your shoulders down and back. Lengthen the back of your neck and tuck your chin slightly. Imagine a string at the top of your head, helping to pull up and lengthen your body. Close your eyes. Breathe here. Feel connected to the earth beneath you.

Tuning Forks: Musicians use tuning forks to tune their instruments. Sound healers have been using tuning forks to transmit sound waves throughout the nervous system to help relieve stress, calm inflammation, and reduce pain.

Binaural Beats: Binaural beats combine two slightly different sound frequencies to create the illusion of one new tone—the difference between the original two tones. Listening to low-frequency tones can trigger a slowdown in brainwave activity that helps you relax, lowers your stress levels, and can help you sleep.

Earthing: Earthing is touching your physical body to the earth. You can walk barefoot through the grass, dirt, mud, or sand. Or sit in the grass with your bare hands touching the earth. Whatever part of the earth you have available to you, touch it with your bare hands or feet. Earthing transfers negatively charged electrons from the earth into your body, neutralizing positively-charged free radicals that cause inflammation. Earthing helps to reduce inflammation in your body, reduces stress, is a potential pain killer, and enhances your immune system. Go be outside, it's pretty awesome.

Try them all, and do what works best for you. Some might be easier for you than others. You might find that one is better to help you sleep, and another is better to help you get through the day. None of these are harmful and can only help you in some way. Enjoy it!

Let's talk about boundaries. A boundary draws the line between you and another. Your boundary is your choice. You get to choose what is good for you and what is not good for you. Having boundaries set in place for yourself and others is a huge step towards giving yourself space and freedom, and not allowing others' yucky energy to stick to you.

You are capable of being aware of others' energies, without taking them on as your own. Once you clear away all the energy that isn't yours, you will get familiar and more comfortable with what your own energy feels like. With practice, you can, on purpose, energetically reach out to feel someone else's energy. You don't have to absorb it and take it as yours, you can just feel it and leave it be. This comes with a reminder: please respect other people's energy space. Just because you can reach out and feel what they are feeling and know what they are going through doesn't give you permission to invade their privacy. Please don't walk up to someone in the supermarket and say, "Hey, it feels like you are going through a divorce. Do you want to talk about it?" Remember to respect your privacy and the privacy of others. Having said that, sometimes spirit nudges you to talk to someone. Connect with them first, and then ask if they want to talk about the issue they are having, or maybe they are ready and open up to you without you having to ask.

As you get more in touch with your own energy, it will get easier for you to notice when you start to feel a little "off."

When you are starting to feel a little "off," that energy might not be yours; it might be someone else's. Ask yourself, "Is this really what I am feeling, or does this energy belong to someone else?" When you take a second to step back and evaluate, it becomes much easier to let go of energy that isn't yours before it all starts to pile on again. Your goal will be to catch it when it first happens, instead of letting it sit and fester.

Lessen the amount of negativity in your life. Many, many years ago, I stopped watching the news. It was one of the healthiest decisions that I have made for myself. Since then, I also cut out TV and movies with too much drama or violence. Mostly, I stick to comedies, romantic comedies, and light-hearted entertainment. Sometimes, I catch a lot of slack for my choices, but I am happy with them. I don't need all that extra negative energy. I don't like feeling it, and it's not something that I need to force myself to do. Why should I force myself to watch a movie that I know won't make me feel good? No, thank you. I will feel what the actors and characters feel, and I just don't need that right now. Your choices are your greatest negativity filter. Some people may not understand your new choices, and that's okay. You are doing what is best for you, and you can feel confident in your decisions.

Resentment is a good indicator of where a boundary should be. If you show up to a party feeling resentful, chances are, you should have turned down the invitation. It's okay. Use it as an opportunity to learn. Next time you feel resentment towards someone or something, take a step back and ask yourself, "Do I really need this in my life?" It's always okay to say no.

If you need to, practice saying no. Make it fun. Stare at yourself in the mirror and say, "No, thank you!" Act like a toddler and run around, saying, "No, no, no!" Then laugh at yourself because that's funny. Seriously, it's always okay to say no. If someone invites you somewhere you know you wouldn't be comfortable, just say no. Allow yourself to say no. It's much better to say no upfront than to say yes, and change your mind at the last minute and cancel. Dragging yourself to the event and being miserable or feeling resentful is just as bad. It's not healthy.

I know it's hard, but saying no is the best way. Another useful tool is to not say yes or no immediately. When someone asks you to commit to something, you can say, "Let me check my schedule and get back to you." This gives you a moment to decide if you really want to do it or if you are over-committing. You will have to get back to them, but then you can say, "No, thank you." I often say, "I'm not able to do that right now, but thank you for asking me!" Sometimes my schedule is actually full, and sometimes my schedule is full of "me time," and that is okay too.

You need to do what's best for you because you won't be able to help other people if you are drowning. It's okay to respect and honor your own needs first, so you can turn around and help others. I know what it's like. You want to help everyone and everything and save the world! I have gone through "save the world" phases. Although it is super productive and helpful, for me, it always ended in exhaustion and burnout. Now, I have limits, and I do what I can do when I can do it, and I still intend to "save the world," but it's in much smaller, more manageable pieces. Like this book. I am helping to save the world by helping you save your world, and for me, that is immensely rewarding. I genuinely want to help you feel better.

Here's one for one of my best friends, and hopefully this helps you too; you don't have to fix everyone or everything. It is not your job. This is a great place for a boundary. Everyone is going through their own mess on their own path. You do not need to bend over backward for everyone you meet throughout life, to fix them and all of their problems. I know it feels like you need to. I know you can. You are very capable. Empaths have this beautiful gift of knowing what other people need, and you can help them.

I'm asking you to be a little pickier and choosey on the number of people you go out of your way for, and the lengths you go through to help them. If you are in the checkout line at the grocery store and someone starts telling you their life story (because that actually happens to empaths), and you suddenly find yourself committing lots of time, money, and energy to helping them, take a step back. Rein it in. Is this what you really want? Are you actually able to follow through with the time, money, and energy commitments? Boundaries.

Here's what I am not saying: I am definitely not saying don't help other people. Helping other people is so natural for us, it can easily turn into, "*I must help everyone, everywhere, all the time!*" Go ahead and help people, but be careful not to give your whole self away. Set limits. Respect your own time and your own energy, and you will be so much more helpful for the fewer people/places/things/animals that you do help.

Physically going shopping is a good place to practice setting boundaries and to remind yourself that you do not need to take on energy that is not yours. When you walk into a store, you can feel the energy of everyone in it, and all of the items in the store. Where the items came from, how many people handled the items, all of the employees, all of the shoppers—it can be overwhelming. It's also a good practice. You can do a quick version of the ground and protect visualization before going in, or you can also practice with a mantra. You can say things like, "I release the energy that is not mine. I let it fall and send it back to the earth with love." Do what works best for you.

One place where I set physical boundaries is at thrift stores. It's really hard on me to be in a place with lots of items that have had multiple previous owners. I feel the leftover energy on the objects. I feel the energy of the previous owners. I feel the energy of the other shoppers, the employees, and then the energy of the store as a whole. It's too uncomfortable for me to feel all of that excess energy, so I generally don't go in. I do love looking at antiques, however, so if I want to go, I make sure I'm already having a good day. I'll do the visualization, and when I am in the store, I am super careful not to let my energy "wander off" and start picking up things I shouldn't. Once you get used to feeling your own energy, it becomes fun to play with and sit back and see what you can feel. For me, an antique store is not the place to practice.

Another suggestion is to set social media and electronic boundaries. It's okay to let your phone go to voicemail, or turn off notifications, or hide your phone for a while. It's okay to take breaks from social media. There is so much information on the internet it can be overwhelming, and I know you can feel all of the energy from everyone you see and everything you look at online. I know you can feel my energy just by reading these words. I hope it's a good experience! It's okay to take that step back, pause, and then move forward with a much narrower field of focus. You can set time limits, or pick one social media site to be on for the day instead of spending hours checking all of them. Put the phone down, close the computer, turn the TV off, turn the screen off, and walk away. Do what you feel you need to do, in that moment.

As you can see, it's so important to have clear boundaries. You will feel better and be healthier. You may also get sick less often and have less physical pain. Remember to respect yourself and respect others. It's always okay to say no. If you can have healthy boundaries, you will be so much better off to help others.

STEP

Two

Release & Let Go

Step 2
Release & Let Go

In Step 2, it's time to forgive, release, and let it go. Forgive yourself for the things you have done or not done, and forgive others for the things they did or didn't do to you. Forgiving someone doesn't mean condoning their behavior or actions and certainly doesn't mean allowing them to do it again. It means giving yourself the freedom to move out of the past and heal for the future.

Even if you forgive someone, it doesn't mean they have to stay in your life. You can forgive and still distance yourself; you don't have to keep them with you. Forgiving someone also takes time, and you may have to remember to forgive again and again as the old feelings come up. It's okay. Choose forgiveness every time, and eventually, the old hurt will be healed and no longer rise to the surface. It will fade away.

Forgiving yourself is usually more difficult than forgiving others. (Sorry.) Guilt, regret, resentment, anger, shame, and sadness can be huge obstacles in forgiving yourself. Allow yourself to sit with those emotions for a little while. See and feel where they are coming from, bring up the memories, cry, laugh, yell, let it all out and say, "I forgive myself." Then repeat it as many times as necessary. Choose to forgive every time.

You can also write out all of your feelings that you wish to release. Write everything down on paper to get it all out. Write anything you want to say to yourself or say to others, anything you feel like you have been holding back or holding onto, or anything that you want to let go. At the end, write something like, "I release these thoughts, feelings, and expressions. I let go of them and release the power they held over me. For my highest good, so it is." Then burn the paper in a safe environment for burning, and allow it to be released. I have done this many times, sometimes for a specific experience that I was trying to overcome, sometimes to help me release a person from my life, and sometimes to release a whole bunch of yuck that I needed to get rid of. It's very helpful. When you are all finished, send yourself some love and accept yourself for who you are—even your mistakes and faults. It may not be okay right now, but it will be. You will get there.

Use those experiences as lessons to learn, take ownership of your actions, and really learn from them and move forward without letting them happen again. Stop the negative self-talk. Notice as soon as your inner monologue turns negative, and stop it in its tracks. You can even say stop, or just put up your hands. Be stern with the negativity, tell it to go, and send yourself more love. Tell yourself something positive, read an affirmation, think of something happy, don't let it get to you, and remember to choose forgiveness. You can say things like "I choose to forgive," or "I choose joy" or "I release the negativity." Remember to be kind to yourself. Be kind to yourself in your actions and in your thoughts. It's always okay to have a bad day or a bad moment. When it's over, regroup and try again. There is no need to beat yourself up. Remember, you matter, and you are worthy of love: love from yourself and love from others.

In your process of forgiving and letting go, remember these things. Not everyone has to like you (you be your best you and let them be them). It's completely okay if someone is mad at you (it may be because they are used to pushing you around instead of you setting healthy boundaries). Your real friends will still love you even when you mess up (if they don't, they are not your real friends, and it's okay to let them go).

How can you let go energetically? By visualizing an energetic cord cutting. What are energetic cords? Energy or etheric cords extend out from your body and connect to other people, places, animals, or objects. The physical distance between you and the person, place, animal, or object doesn't matter; you can feel it across the world. Have you ever felt like you have a strange attachment to something, and you don't know why? It's probably because of an energetic cord. An energetic cord is also how you can tell if you like someone before you actually meet them.

Energy flows through thought, and you can create a cord just by thinking about someone. Even a short interaction can create a temporary cord that vanishes once your interaction is over. Or if you have a longer, more involved relationship, the cord is larger and stronger. Your strongest cords (for better or for worse) are from those relationships that are closest to you. You can also have cords that connect you to deceased relatives.

What is cord cutting? An energetic cord cutting cuts or severs the ties that connect you to another person, place, object, or experience. A cord cutting can be beneficial to a relationship to help release negative energies that you are holding onto. Cord cuttings don't have to be a bad disconnection if you perform them with love and have healing intentions. Cord cuttings allow the negative energy to fall away and make room for more positive energy and healthy relationships.

Some cords are more difficult to cut, it may take a few visualizations to actually release the energy. Sometimes, you may not be able to cut the cord because you are tied to that person karmically. That karma needs to play out and be released before the cord can disappear. If you are having a hard time moving on from something or someone, it's a good idea to do a cord cutting. You can also bring up a memory and cut the cord between you and the memory to help you move on.

If you are performing a cord cutting, know that it's okay to send someone's energy back to them. You can acknowledge their energy and send it back with love. It's not yours. Everyone has their own path, and you can still help them, but carrying their burden is not helpful to them in the long run. They need to walk their own path. Empower them, don't enable them.

When I am finished with a Reiki session, in-person or distance, I will always visualize the energetic cord that was created, cut it with love and send the other person's energy back with love and gratitude. If I forget to do that, I will continue to feel their energy, just as if they were standing in the room with me telling me about their day and how they feel. I will also continue to receive messages from spirit for them. For me, it's incredibly important to cut the cord, so I don't take on someone else's energy and continue to feel them after the session has ended.

I'd like to talk for a minute about the mother/child connection. I'll share a personal story with you. A few years ago, my son's energy was driving me crazy. All I knew was that I felt it, and I didn't like it. I was going to go insane. I was new to the empath scene and didn't know what I was doing. I had just learned about energy cords and cord cuttings. Energy cords are something that I had felt but didn't have a name for them. I posted in a group about my son's energy grating me. I was at my wit's end and was thinking about doing a cord cutting, but I wasn't sure if it was the right thing to do.

My post caused some backlash. Some of the comments were helpful, and some of them were pretty angry. A few people said a cord cutting would permanently ruin our relationship and mother/son connection for the rest of our lives. Some of it was fear-based (Now, I can easily spot and walk away from other people projecting their fears on me.). Those people were speaking from their experiences, but it was a little overwhelming for me. It was then that an angel in the group "pulled me aside" and took me under her wing to help me through the things that I was going through. It wasn't totally about my son's energy, but also about the baggage that I was carrying and emotions that I was dealing with. She helped me through those things, and I did not do the cord cutting.

I believe the mother/child connection is special and not to be taken lightly. Since then, I have found another technique that I think is very helpful to turn down the noise while you work through your own issues and baggage. Instead of cutting the cord, visualize flipping a switch, closing a door, or shutting a window. The cord is still there, but you are practicing self-care and telling your body and soul that you need some time to be with your own energy. You can still see your child's energy, but it's not so loud and intrusive. The mother/child energy line is incredibly powerful and should be respected and treated with care. If you find yourself in a similar situation, I hope this helps you.

Cord Cutting Visualization

Begin by sitting or lying down comfortably. Relax your mind, and relax your muscles. Let it go. Take a release breath, inhale through your nose, and open your mouth to release. Close your eyes, and take two more release breaths.

Continue to relax your body, breathe normally, and pull your attention towards your breath. Breathe here a few breaths. Begin to feel heavy and connected to the earth. See roots coming out from your feet and traveling down, deep into the earth.

Feel the earth's warm and comforting energy. Pull the earth's energy up through the roots and see it surrounding your whole body from below your feet to above your head. See a beautiful, large bright ball of energy around your body. Feel safe and protected.

Take another release breath, inhale through your nose, and open your mouth to release.

See the energetic cord that connects you to the person, place, object, or experience that you wish to sever. Where is it connected to your body? How large or small is it? What color is it? See it clearly. Follow it. How long or short is it? Follow its flow to the person, place, object, or experience. See how it's connected to them.

See a large pair of scissors, or a knife, or a sword, or another object that works for you. See it in your hands. Pull loving energy up from the roots from your feet, up through your body. See the loving energy move from your hands into the object. Say to yourself, "I cut this cord that connects me to (name the person, place, object, or experience) with love and healing, for my highest good." See them clearly in your mind's eye, see the cord, feel the loving energy flowing from your body into the scissors or other objects.

Take a deep breath in. See yourself cutting the cord. See the cord separate into two pieces. See your end of the cord come back into your body and surround the connection location with love and healing energy. See the other piece of the cord go back to them, send it love, and help push it away.

Take a release breath, inhale through your nose, and open your mouth to release. Say to yourself, "I release the cord and the energy that had connected me, with love and healing, for my highest good, and so it is."

Take another release breath. Inhale through your nose, and open your mouth to release. See yourself brushing off the excess energy around you. Brush it off, and let it fall back into the earth. Remain connected to the earth beneath you. Feel grounded, strong, and steady. Bring more loving energy up from the earth through the roots, up through your body, and place it in your heart. Put your hands over your heart. Say to yourself, "I love you." Smile.

Take one last release breath, inhale through your nose, and open your mouth to release. Open your eyes. How do you feel? How did it go? I hope it worked beautifully for you.

If you would like to hear that visualization on YouTube, it's at: https://youtu.be/m37YaASzTro.

Energetic cords can be positive or negative, and information transfers both ways. You are not just the receiver; you also send energy to the other person. With that, let's talk about energy vampires. Energy vampires are people who drain you of your energy. They feed on your compassion, kindness, and caring nature, and leave you feeling exhausted. They come in all shapes and sizes. They can zap your energy on purpose, or sometimes they have no idea they are doing it—it just happens.

To identify an energy vampire, the easiest question to ask yourself is: how do you feel when you are around them? Do you feel happy, upbeat, and positive? Do you feel tired, nauseous, sad, or suddenly in a bad mood? Do you feel vulnerable or confused? If you consistently don't feel good after talking to them or being around them, they are probably an energy vampire. Being an empath is like a giant beacon for energy vampires and narcissists (more on them later). They are drawn to you because you listen, you are kind, and you can see the good in everyone. There is good in everyone, but not everyone is good for you. You have a beautiful, bright light inside of you broadcasting to the world. Not everyone that is drawn to your light will be good for you.

Please stay away from these people. It might be someone in your inner circle or a family member. It might be difficult to put some distance between you and them, but for your safety, sanity, and general health, please try to keep them at arm's length. Try avoiding them completely, or have very limited interaction with them. If you have to talk to them, recognize the situation, and don't feed into their drama. This means they cannot be your sounding board for advice or drama, and you cannot react to whatever it is they are spouting. Put up your protections, and get very stoic, let them say their piece, then say "yep" and walk away. Or whatever works for you. Back away, walk away, don't get involved. You can also tell them you are tired and aren't able to meet with them or talk to them, or whatever it is they are asking of you. If you are tired, they won't want to be around you because they can't feed off your energy. It's okay to let them go.

Remember, abuse is never okay. Only a toxic person will tell you to overlook it or let it go. Set strong boundaries with that toxic person and understand that no form of abuse is okay. Whether it's emotional or physical abuse, it is not okay under any circumstance. Know your worth. You are worth so much more than keeping quiet and tolerating any kind of abuse. Stay strong in your boundaries too. The abuser and any other toxic person in your life will tell you to let it happen and to stay quiet about it. Listen to my words and, more importantly, listen to your heart. You do not deserve to be abused. You are worthy. Leave them behind.

Let's talk more about casually letting people slide out of your life. While you are "in the thick of things" during your healing, you might want to let activities and people go. You can pick up some activities at a later point when you feel ready, but while you are in the middle of it all, it's completely okay to let it go. First, let go of the energy vampires and the narcissists. The other people that you may want to distance yourself from are generally negative people who are full of drama. You just don't need that in your life right now.

Here are a few reminders to help you on your journey. You are not responsible for someone else's thoughts and actions; everyone has their own path and their own baggage. You walk your own path and let everyone else walk theirs. Let go of the drama. It's okay not to get involved in someone else's baggage. Take a step back and see it for what it is—unnecessary negativity that you don't need to take on as yours. You don't have to give the situation, or them, your energy. You are completely responsible for your own thoughts, emotions, and actions. If it feels as if someone is forcing you to do something, recognize it, back away, and change your perspective. Your reactions to someone or something are your choice. Drop the drama. It's okay; you can do it.

Different people have different opinions. None are right or wrong. It's okay to believe what you believe. You can't force other people to believe the same thing that you do. Accept that you are different in that way and move on. It's okay to be different. Listen to your heart and speak your truth. It's okay to disagree with someone. I'll say it again: *It's okay to disagree with someone or not to follow their advice.* It's okay to not follow my advice!

Do what feels right for you, and do what is best for you, no matter who is making the suggestion. At the end of the day, you are responsible for your own life and your choices. You have to live with the decisions that you have made. It's always okay to disagree. You can be you and let them be them. You can still be friends and be respectful and have different viewpoints and opinions. It's okay to agree to disagree.

> Tip: In the shower, imagine the water is cleansing your energy, washing away the negativity, and the excess energy that doesn't belong to you.

STEP

Three

Practice Self Care

Step 3
Practice Self Care

Self-care: the good, the bad, and the ugly. Self-care is one of the most important steps in this book. If you aren't taking the time to care for yourself, you won't be able to care for others. It's that simple. Please, give yourself permission and take the time to care for yourself. It's always okay to take the time to fill your cup, or at least make sure it's not completely empty. I know it's hard to find the time, I understand. We will talk about self-care techniques that take very little time and money.

For a long while, I ran on fumes. My plate was full, and my cup was empty. That was an incredibly hard time in my life. Each morning, it was so hard to get up. It was hard to get things done. Even the smallest tasks were hard. Everything felt so heavy. Everything is temporary. It passed, I got through it, and carving out the time for self-care was unbelievably helpful and necessary. If you do nothing else in this book, please start caring for yourself now. Give yourself permission to do the things that you want to do and then actually do them. Practicing self-care will help you find your joy.

Everyone is always going, going, going. Do this, do that, go, go, go! Take a break. Take a breath. Take time to slow down and listen to your heart. Take a whole day and bum around the house. (I am not able to do this one very often. It's extremely rare, but oh boy, it's one of my favorites!) There is nothing wrong with that. It's okay to be lazy sometimes. If you take care of yourself, then you are better equipped to take care of those around you.

At some point along the way, I realized that I had never given myself permission to feel what I truly felt. I was riddled with guilt, calling myself lazy for needing to rest or take time off or do anything for myself. It was incredibly calming to lay down and let go of all of the guilt and negative thoughts about myself. It's okay to rest. It's okay to take time off, to slow down, and to say no. It's okay to do whatever it is that you need to do and to feel what you need to feel. Fill your cup. I give you permission to fill your cup. Now you have to give yourself permission. Let go of your expectations and take time for self-care.

Make the time for sleep and rest. There will forever be plenty of reasons not to. If that means something else in your life slides for a bit or becomes a lower priority, so be it. Whatever amount of sleep that your body needs, get it. Say no to invites for events, and no to extra projects. Say no to the dishes, the dusting. Let the laundry go for another day. At the end of the day, as soon as you can, you get into bed and get the amount of sleep your body needs. If you can sleep and drink more water than you think you need, that will propel you in the right direction.

If you are one who is already sleeping excessively, definitely do the ground and protect visualization regularly. It will help keep you from piling on everyone else's energy. Also, Step 6, "Go Within and Seek Your Answers," will be very helpful for you because your body is already telling you to do that. Resist the urge to skip right to that section. There are only seven steps; they are all necessary!

If it doesn't feel right, don't do it. It's okay to say no to doing things because you need time for self-care. If you aren't already caring for yourself, you will need to steal that time from somewhere. Beginning to say "no" and not overscheduling yourself is a great start.

Sometimes you need extra energy, you are running on empty, and you need to practice self-care, or just get yourself through the day. If you want to amplify your energy, effectively revving up your engine, you can create an energy circle. Remember, this will help you short term, and is not a replacement for self-care! Sometimes, you just need to take a nap. Give your body what it needs, or it will get it by any means (like you getting really sick).

To create an energy circle or loop, sit quietly and take a few deep breaths. Use a quick grounding visual. See the etheric cords come out from your feet and go into the ground and wrap around the Earth's core. Clasp your hands together, or interlace your fingers and place your hands on top of your head, and cross your feet at your ankles. You have now created a physical boundary for your energy. Your hands and feet are crossed.

Close your eyes. Imagine your energy as a stream of light. Give it a color, and give it a texture. See the stream of light running up one side of your body as you breathe in, and down the other side of your body as you breathe out. See it fully completing the loop around your body, from your head all the way to your toes. As you gain energy, you can see the light going faster and faster. Keep your breath steady, only the energy goes faster.

When you are ready, see the light going into your belly at your solar plexus chakra. Place your hands on your solar plexus, calm your breath, and relax. If you feel disjointed or out of sorts, ground yourself again. Thank yourself for taking the time to help you feel better. This is a great exercise to do in the mornings when you need to get going. Remember to use it as an additional tool, and not in place of other self-care methods.

Remembering to practice self-care can be hard. This is where I have trouble. I get caught up in everyday life, and when things get hard, I put my head down and push through. I keep going at any expense. I tell myself that this situation is temporary, and if I can get through it to the other side, everything will be better. I forget that if I were to do a short meditation while lying in bed right before attempting to fall asleep, I would sleep better and be more prepared to handle all the crap that comes at me during the day. I forget that if I take 15 minutes or an hour to do something for me, I will feel like my plate isn't so full, even though it is.

I will be better equipped to handle it all and maybe even in a better mindset to realize that not everything on my plate is important, and some of it can go. You don't have to be a bull in a china shop going through life. You don't have to be laser-focused to "get through" while you continuously take hits from all around you. Take a few minutes to breathe fresh air, or to notice the beauty around you, or to meditate, or do something bigger that gets you out of your daily routine. You will thank yourself afterward. You don't have to do it alone. You always have this book, this support group (www.facebook.com/groups/beginnerempath), and of course, you have your higher self and your team of spirit guides. They are always here for you, even if you can't see or hear them. Find ways to make your life easier.

Somehow, I got attached to the slogan, "grin and bear it." I let others treat me like shit, and I treated myself like shit. I talked badly to my body, and if I were uncomfortable or wasn't happy, I would tell myself to grin and bear it. You don't have to just "get through" life. You can change the smallest things and be so much happier.

Let's make a list of all the things that you could do to care for yourself. Some can be quick, easy, and free. Some can be more time consuming, cost a little money, or a lot of money; just put it on your list. I've done this. I can tell you it will help! When you are feeling overwhelmed or maxed out or drained, you need more self-care. Take a look at your list and see what you can do immediately. It can be as easy as closing your eyes to take a few deep breaths. Breathing is free and easy. You can do it.

You can also spend 10 minutes outside, doing nothing, just breathing fresh air. Some of my favorites are having acupuncture, digital painting, hanging out with close friends, lying in bed and staring at the ceiling (seriously), sleeping, going for a drive in the car (ideally with the windows down and music up), taking yoga classes and sitting on the beach.

You can have seasonal self-care activities like skiing or hiking. Make your list and keep it accessible. Put it on your phone, on the fridge, or wherever else you look frequently. Remind yourself to look at it to make sure you are doing something for you. When you don't feel like practicing self-care and you don't want to add to your to-do list, that's when you absolutely need self-care the most. Make the time. It will help you. You will feel better.

Another key to self-care is the way you speak to yourself. Use kind words when you think about yourself. I had heard this a lot before and always brushed it off. I always said mean things to myself. How ugly I was, how much I hated my back for hurting all the time, how I hated my pudgy belly, how I wasn't good at anything, how much I hated being tired all of the time, how I hated my life, how I was a jack of all trades but didn't excel anywhere. I could go on.

You can see how I spoke to myself; it was so negative. (Also, doing shadow work will help you love those things that you think you hate about yourself. Shadow work is in Step 6.) I absolutely did not believe that thinking nice thoughts about myself would help. Well, you can add that to the list of things that I have been wrong about because it does work! Be kind to yourself. Speak kindly to yourself. Think nice thoughts. When you start to say something bad about yourself, stop in mid-thought or mid-sentence, just stop. Acknowledge that it was not healthy behavior and move on to something more positive.

I'm not saying to avoid negative things. Acknowledge the negative and move on from it. There is no need to dwell on it and speak negatively about yourself. If there are things you aren't so good at and need to work on, acknowledge that you need to improve those areas and then work on them. Encourage yourself instead of telling yourself how bad it is. Practicing self-care means caring for yourself, caring about the way you speak to yourself, and caring about the way you treat yourself.

Sometimes self-care isn't a "fun" activity. Sometimes self-care is "ugly." Sometimes, it's doing the necessary things in life, like putting the laundry away or de-cluttering your space (after you get the proper amount of sleep, of course). Sometimes self-care is being an adult and creating boundaries. It's doing what feels right, instead of what looks right. Listen to your heart as you create your list.

I've created a list of suggested items. Feel free to use some of these, or throw them out. Remember to do what feels right for you. There is also a page at the end of the book for you to write down your own self-care ideas, and what works best for you. Feel free to make notes!

Self-Care Ideas:

Take deep breaths, put your hand on your heart and listen, smile, sleep, relax, bum around the house, be lazy, get cozy, say "No," meditate, stare at the ceiling, take yoga, qigong, tai-chi, get acupuncture, read affirmations, read books you love, write, write down your boundaries, say nice things to yourself, make a list of things that you are good at, spend time alone, eat healthy foods, make a list of things you are grateful for, dance, go outside, go for a drive, go to the beach, travel, exercise, walk, run, jump, climb, ski, hike, get a massage, create a digital painting, paint, create or paint pottery, create something, take a class, hang out with friends, visit family, laugh, drink a lot more water, clean your space, de-clutter your space, take a bath, listen to music, play an instrument, or try a new healing modality. There are a lot of different types of healing modalities out there, and we will talk about those in the next step.

If part of your self-care is meditation and visualization, you can always retreat to your happy place. Here is a guided visualization to help get you there:

Begin by taking a comfortable seat. Either on the floor or in a chair. Or you can lay flat on your back with your knees bent and your feet on the ground. Breathe here. Start to notice your breath. Pay attention to how fast or slow it is. Feel your belly rise and fall as you inhale and exhale. Take a release breath here, inhale through your nose, exhale through your mouth. Take another release breath, inhale through your nose, exhale through your mouth.

Let go of the tension and stress in your body. Relax. Let your thoughts go. If you have random thoughts that come in, think them and let them go. Move on. Continue focusing on your breath. Feel your belly rise and fall, with each inhale and exhale. Breathe here.

Now imagine you are in your favorite place. Find that favorite place that you have. Maybe no one knows about it. Your favorite place that you like to go to. Maybe it's even a place that you have never visited, but you imagine what it's like. Is it warm? Is it cold? Is it sunny or cloudy? Inside or outside? You pick. Be there. Feel the weather. Is it raining or snowing? Is the sun shining? Are you indoors? Be where you need to be. Continue breathing. Inhaling through your nose, exhaling through your nose. Relax in your safe space.

This is your place. Feel safe here. Comfortable. At home. Feel peaceful. Know that you can come back here at anytime, anywhere. This is your safe space. Continue focusing on your breath. Relaxing your body. Imagining your safe space. Your favorite place. Continue breathing in through your nose and out through your nose. Imagining your safe space. Feeling relaxed and content—peaceful.

Now walk outside of your safe space in your mind. What's it like outside of your safe space? Is it sunny? Is it cloudy? Is it raining? Can you hear the birds? Is it completely quiet? What's directly outside of your safe space, your favorite place? Walk around. Enjoy the space outside. As you imagine it, feel the weather. Is it sunny? Is it warm? Is it cold? Are you shivering? Continue breathing in through your nose and out through your nose, taking long breaths. Walk around, just outside of your safe space, in your mind. Noticing things outside. Are there rocks? Are there rivers? Is there water? Mountains? What's it like?

Continue taking slow deep breaths, in through your nose, out through your nose. Walking around outside your safe space. Now relax your mind. Letting it go, letting the visualization go. Letting go of your thoughts, keeping your body relaxed. Bringing your awareness back into your body. Coming back to center, coming back to earth. Feeling grounded, where you physically sit or lay. Coming back into your body. Be here, be present in this moment.

Take three release breaths. Inhale through your nose, open your mouth, and release. Two more. Inhale through your nose, open your mouth, and release. The last one, inhale through your nose, open your mouth and release. Let it all go. Let the stress fade away. Let the worry melt away. Let any negativity bounce off of you. Let it all go. Let it wash away. Feel calm and rested and peaceful. You can open your eyes and begin again.

If you would like to listen to this guided visualization, you can find it here on YouTube:
https://youtu.be/XrjhTWL8s_8.

STEP

Four

Try Different Healing Modalities

Step 4
Try Different Healing Modalities

Trying different healing modalities goes hand in hand with self-care. Any type of healing you try fills your cup and heals your soul. Attempt meditation, try reiki, try past life regression workshops, acupuncture, massage, yoga, chakra healings, Qigong, Tai Chi, spiritual recovery, see a spiritual therapist, or try something not on this list, try it all and see what works for you. Find your local "hippy center" or spiritual center or wellness center, and start going there. I worked for a wellness center, and it helped to heal my soul. I took yoga classes, I went through yoga teacher training, I meditated, I taught yoga and meditation, I had acupuncture and massage all the time, I was Reiki level 1 certified, and I participated in events. It was a fantastic start to my healing journey. I met an amazing group of people and still keep in touch with many of them today.

Years later, I found another location for classes and events, and it took my healing to the next level. I was Reiki level 2 and 3 certified, I took yoga classes, I took crystal meditation classes and had Reiki healing sessions. I even participated in classes just because I was curious.

I believe in reincarnation, I believe that we live this life for a purpose, to learn something and for our souls to grow.

When we die, we can hang out in the spirit world for a while and choose our next life to be born into. (That's the short and sweet version.)

I saw a past life regression workshop on the schedule and felt drawn to it. (Side note—follow your intuition! If you feel drawn to something, if it's healthy and not harmful, try it!) So, I tried it, and had this beautiful, amazing experience! I already knew about two of my past lives, and she walked me through two more that I had never experienced before. It opened the door to some amazing healing! Everyone's experience is different, and everyone has their own path to walk, but boy did this help me. We all hold trauma from past lives. It could be from something that we didn't learn or something that we didn't let go of. I believe that empaths are especially sensitive to the weight of a past life and can easily pile it on like it's still happening today. It's okay to let it all go.

You can also try sound healing. Some practitioners use tuning forks (like we saw in Step 1) to transmit sound waves throughout the nervous system to help relieve stress, calm inflammation and reduce pain. You can also search for binaural beats (also from Step 1) and solfeggios. There are lots of free videos to watch on YouTube. There is also a popular movement for tones and music at 432 Hz, which matches the natural musical pitch of the universe and is supposed to be good for spiritual development. Some practitioners use singing bowls, which reduces stress and anxiety, lowers blood pressure, improves circulation, and can promote pain relief and chakra balancing.

Here's another example of trying something different. I met with a woman who walked me through a unique visualization. She had me see my spirit animals. I knew I was kind of connected with two animals. I had always felt drawn to them, so when she asked me to see my spirit animals, they popped right into my head. She took me on a journey through a visualization and asked me to take my spirit animals with me. At the end of the visualization, she asked me to take the spirit animals into my body, wrapping my arms around them and accepting them as part of me. It was amazing. I had never felt so whole and so complete in my entire life. It was like something was missing throughout my life, and I had just found it. I'm tearing up right now just thinking about it. It was beautiful. I was grateful for the experience. Try as many different kinds of healing techniques as you possibly can. There is a page at the end of the book for you to write down different healing modalities that you want to try.

Let's talk about meditation. Meditation is a heightened state of awareness where you become one with your inner self and everything around you at the same time. Meditation uses different techniques to allow you to quiet your mind and reach down into your soul. It will help you gain focus, clarity, and peace. It can help you answer questions that you have by giving you the opportunity to listen to your inner self (your intuition). You already know the answers, you just have to access them. It also allows you to see your thoughts and feelings from a different perspective and without judgment.

Now, I do say "attempt" meditation. It's okay if you fail or are terrible at it, or don't like it. If that's the case, just sit quietly, and that by itself will help you greatly. You can try meditation classes in person. You can try meditation online. If you feel connected to me, you can find me on YouTube by searching for Healing Light Empath. You can try meditation in books, or you can try sitting quietly and doing what feels best for you. Try it all, do what you feel drawn to do. Do whatever feels right. There are so many different kinds of meditations and meditation techniques. Pick one, and start there. Here are a few types to help get you going.

Mindfulness meditation – Observing your thoughts and emotions and letting them pass without judgment, you are intentionally focusing fully on the present moment. You don't have to sit quietly to do this, it can be during your everyday activity, just be focused on whatever it is that you are doing. If you want to sit quietly, you can then allow your thoughts to come and go and focus on your breath.

Mantra meditation – A mantra is a rhythmic repetition of a sacred sound or phrase. Mantra practice can calm the mind and bring the practitioner into a one-pointed state of awareness. The sound uses vibrations to energize and transform the brain and nervous system. This one also works great if you are having trouble falling asleep. Using the rhythmic chanting is very helpful. The chant I use is "Om Gam Ganapataye Namaha," which is a chant to Ganesh, who is the remover of all obstacles. I set the intention that he will remove my obstacles for sleep, and sing the chant in my head. It works great for me. Hopefully, it works for you too!

Guided meditation – Using visualization techniques with your imagination to invoke your senses, sight in your mind, smells, tastes, and sounds. It provides a new atmosphere to calm and relax you. You can also use affirmations during your guided meditation. This is one of my favorites. Being guided through a visualization can be very relaxing, and you don't have to worry about where you are going or what to do, you just let it go and go with the flow.

Chakra meditation – A chakra is an energy point (cluster of nerves) along the main energy channel that flows from the upper brain down to the base of your spine. It regulates your physical, mental, and emotional states. Seven major chakras run up your spine to the top of your head. Each chakra has a corresponding color and mantra, and you can focus on the colors and repeat the mantras to help open your chakras.

Music meditation – Where you focus on calming nature music or Native American drumming or flute music, something that helps to relax you and be at peace. You can let your thoughts drift away while you focus on the music, letting everything else go.

Crystal meditation – You can use crystals to help you meditate for a specific outcome. The vibrations of the crystals also help facilitate the state of meditation. Depending on which crystals you choose, they can help in different ways like calming your mind, improving your focus, releasing anger or fear, or promoting new beginnings.

This is nowhere near a complete list of meditation techniques, but it's a good start. I want to give you the basic tools and let you run with it. See where it takes you! Let's try a chakra meditation. This is a well-rounded meditation for clearing your chakras and getting you to focus on your breath. This will also help you to get some of that excess energy out that might not be yours. You can do it!

Start by sitting or lying comfortably. Take three release breaths first. Inhale deeply through your nose, all the way. Keep going until your lungs are full, open your mouth and let it all out. Two more. Inhale, slowly and completely, filling your lungs all the way, open your mouth, and release. The last one, inhale through your nose, slowly, fully, deeply, and open your mouth to release, let it all go. Nice job. Now, take a minute to just follow your own breath. Relax. Let it go. Release your expectations. Focus on your breath. Feel your belly rise and fall as you inhale and exhale. Allow your body to melt into your seat. Be still. Finish reading this sentence and then close your eyes for a little bit to just listen and feel your breath. Go ahead. When you are ready, open your eyes and we will begin.

Take a deep breath in and imagine your Root Chakra (Muladhara Chakra). It's located at the bottom of your spine along the perineum. See the color red, vibrant, and swirling. Imagine it getting larger and spinning around and around. This is where you are rooted. Feel connected to the earth beneath you, feel grounded and safe. Send it love. Breathe here.

Take a deep breath in and imagine your Sacral Chakra (Svadisthana Chakra), it's located about two inches below your belly button inside the soft spot. See the color orange, vibrant, and swirling. Imagine it getting larger and spinning around and around. This is where you feel: feel pleasure, and abundance. Feel the energy of your body. Feel it expand and contract as you breathe. Feel complete and whole. Send it love. Breathe here.

Take a deep breath in and imagine your Solar Plexus Chakra (Manipura Chakra). It's located at your solar plexus muscle, just below your ribs. See the color yellow, vibrant, and swirling. Imagine it getting larger and spinning around and around. This is where you "do." Feel the abundance of power running through your body. Feel active and ready to go. Send the bright yellow chakra love. Breathe here.

Take a deep breath in and imagine your Heart Chakra (Anahata Chakra). It's located at your heart center in your chest. See the color green, vibrant, and swirling. Imagine it getting larger and spinning around and around. This is where you love! Feel the love of the universe surrounding you! Feel it's warm, brilliant, green light in your chest, expanding and surrounding your whole body with love and light. Send yourself some love. Tell yourself, "I love you exactly as you are." Breathe here.

Take a deep breath in and imagine your Throat Chakra (Vishuddha Chakra). It's located at the base of your throat. See the color blue, vibrant, and swirling. Imagine it getting larger and spinning around and around. This is where you speak. Free your voice. Allow yourself to communicate freely and openly. Allow you to be you. Imagine pulling the lump in your throat out to clear the blockage. Find your words. Send your throat love. Breathe here.

Take a deep breath in and imagine your Third Eye Chakra (Ajna Chakra). It's located between your eyebrows. See the color indigo, vibrant, and swirling. Imagine it getting larger and spinning around and around. This is where you know. You already know the answers. Give yourself the time and space to see them. Allow yourself to see. Open your mind. Send your third eye love. Breathe here.

Take a deep breath in and imagine your Crown Chakra (Sahasrara Chakra); it's located just above the top of your head. See the color violet, vibrant, and swirling. Imagine it getting larger and spinning around and around. This is where you understand. Become connected to the universe and all the love and positivity that is out there. Feel yourself expanding. Understand that everything is connected. We are all different yet the same: plants, animals, people, nature, science. We are all equal and connected. Send your crown chakra some love. Breathe here.

Begin to come back to center, come back to your breath, come back into your body. Come back. Take one more release breath (or more if you like). Inhale through your nose, deeply, slowly, all the way in, and exhale through your mouth, letting it all go. Close your eyes for a minute, and imagine dusting yourself off, letting go of the excess. Brush it off. Feel grounded as you sit for a little longer to come out of your meditation. Smile. I hope you feel great. Be proud of yourself for taking the time to clear your chakras and heal your soul.

That is just one of many meditations out there. I truly hope that was helpful for you, and you can come back and practice as often as you would like.

I hope you can try as many different healing modalities as possible. Find local events and places. Find healing online (as long as it's a trusted source. Please do not give away all your money to someone making big promises and do not get mixed up with people who say there is a curse on you and they will remove it… please try not to get scammed). You can heal yourself. No one else can do it for you. Other people have tools that help you, but you are the one doing the work. That's another reason I love Reiki.

Reiki is an energy tool that practitioners use to help you to heal yourself. It's like a massage for your energy. Everyone heals their bodies differently, and at their own pace. Reiki is non-harming; it will only benefit you to your highest good. I am a Master Reiki Practitioner, and if you would like to set up a distance healing session, I am happy to send you energy to help you heal yourself. (Link for scheduling: https://schedulehealinglightempath.as.me/schedule.php) It's just another way. In the end, it's your path, and you have to travel it. I hope you find something that helps you along the way.

STEP

Five

Find Your Tribe

Step 5
Find Your Tribe

It's incredibly important to have people in your life who understand you and what you are going through. Even if some of them are only online, people just like you, live all over the world. You might find that you need to distance yourself from some of your friends and even family. If your current friends or even close family are very negative, bring lots of drama, talk badly about you, or are mean to you, then it's time to let them go and create a little more space between you. You don't have to cut them out of your life completely, but definitely put some distance between you.

It will do you a world of good to find people, locally and online, who believe the same things that you believe. There is something to be said for having friends with common interests and activities. People who don't think that you're crazy. When you go through all of this, it's easy to think that you are crazy, especially if there is a narcissist in your life who is gaslighting you.

Side note: A narcissist is someone who has exaggerated feelings of importance, who lacks empathy for others, who always insists that they are right, is manipulative and willing to exploit others. They seek attention or admiration. They do not accept healthy criticism, and they believe the world owes them something. A narcissist will never see you as their equal. In general, they blame you for everything. Gaslighting is when one person, or group, manipulates another person, or group, by making them question their own reality. The person using gaslighting will deny that something ever happened, or lie about the severity of the situation.

They will destabilize someone's beliefs, making them question their own memories, perceptions, or sanity. If there is someone in your life doing this to you—RUN. GO. Go in the other direction, leave them, give them so much space they wonder where you are and why they can't manipulate you anymore. They will try to keep you, to continue to manipulate you. They will say awful things to get you to stay. Go. Find your strength, take your power back, and go. Emotional abuse can be just as damaging as physical abuse. Just because this person is not hitting you does not mean they are not abusing you. There are many resources for people leaving abusive relationships. You are not alone. You are not crazy. You are strong. The National Domestic Violence Hotline number is 1-800-799-7233. If you are in an abusive relationship, please reach out for help. It's always okay to ask for help.

Remember, you are not crazy. Find people that you can talk to and say the things that are in your heart and in your head. You know they are true, speak your truth. In Step 4, I suggested finding your local "hippy center." If you haven't done that already, go search for it now. Make friends with other people that go there whom you are drawn to. Start with one person. If you can have one other person to tell the craziest-sounding things in your head, you will feel so much better. They will probably share the crazy-sounding things in their head too. It will be beautiful.

Go to your local "hippy center," spiritual center or wellness center, try activities and join groups, meet people. You are not alone. You just haven't found your people yet. In fact, you are never alone because your spirit guides are always with you. You have a whole team of beautiful beings here to help you through this crazy life journey. They are already communicating with you; you just need to stop and listen. Pay attention to them.

Let's go on a little tangent for a minute and talk about these Spirit Guides. You can call them Angels, Archangels, Guardian Angles, Spirits, Ancestors, Ascended Masters, Spirit Animals, Elementals, Enlightened Beings, Gods and Goddesses, Sacred Elders, or another name if you have one. Some people believe that you, as a currently living person, can be a spirit guide for someone else, either here on earth or another faraway planet or another plane of existence.

Your Spirit Guides are always here to help you, and you can always ask them for help. Talking to your Spirit Guides can become so second nature that you talk out loud to them, you can see them with your third eye, you can feel them, and you can hear them. Some Guides may come and go, when you need them, and some are meant to be with you throughout your entire life. They showed up at birth, or even before you were born, and they will stay with you.

Your Guides love you unconditionally. They love all parts of you. They are beings of light and of love. They want to help you make it through life, to enjoy life, to help enlighten you, to show you your true path, to help you become your true self, to bring you peace, and to show you kindness. They help to heal your past life trauma and generational trauma, they help you find balance, and they push you to grow.

They are trying to communicate with you. How do you listen? How do you connect with your Spirit Guides? The first step to connecting with your Guides is to just start talking to them. Tell them that you are open to receiving guidance and communication. You can also be direct and tell them the best ways to communicate with you. You can tell them that they need to keep repeating communications because you might not see it for the first 50 times. You can tell them that communication needs to hit you on the head and be incredibly obvious. You might actually get hit on the head, so be careful what you wish for.

When I first started listening to my Guides, songs were the easiest way for them to communicate with me. I would hear a song and just know that it was them. If that happens to you, tell them that you got the message, and encourage more of that kind of communication. They may also communicate through repeating numbers, like 111, 1111, 222, 333, etc. Or it could be a seemingly random number, but it means something special to you.

Once, I had an experience where I saw what I thought was a random number, but I heard and felt this powerful noise and shaking, almost like thunder, but the weather was clear. I saw this number and heard/felt this energy, and I just knew that number was meant for me. There are lots of websites where you can look up what these Angel numbers or Spiritual numbers mean, read them, and see your message.

You can ask your Guides a question, just before you fall asleep and ask them to respond through your dreams. In the morning, write down what you remember and see if your answer is in there. You can also talk to your Spirit Guides and ask them to communicate with you while you are in meditation. Sometimes, you will hear or feel their answers or guidance as an inner knowing. Sometimes, you just "know." You don't know how you know, and you can't really explain it, but you just "know." *Listen.* This is your Guide trying to communicate with you.

The more you listen, and the more you follow their guidance, the more it will happen, and the easier it will be. If you hear/see/feel their guidance and don't follow through, you won't receive the guidance as often. Keep listening, keep trusting, keep your faith, and follow through. They are only here to help you. Remember to thank your Guides. Thank them often. Send them love, you can even see yourself hugging them. Hug your Spirit Guides. They have helped you through a lot. Talk to them anytime you want. They are here for you, always.

Let's get back to it. If you live in a location that doesn't have a "hippy center," you can rely on your spirit guides and the people online. Or you can create your own local group of people who sit around sharing the "crazy," you just need to find them.

If you are looking for resources online, I have a few already started. These resources are a great way to connect to other people like you, share stories, read articles, and be completely yourself. You can see what I'm up to at: HealingLightEmpath.com or find support at: facebook.com/groups/BeginnerEmpath

Here is a guided meditation to help you clear away old energies and set an intention to bring in new, positive energies, people, and experiences into your life.

Begin by sitting or lying down comfortably. Pay attention to your breath, just focus on it without changing it in any way. Start to relax your muscles. Let the tension melt away. Relax your eyes. Relax your mouth. Relax your jaw. Keep your focus on your breath. Slow down your breathing and take long inhales and long exhales. Close your eyes and focus on breathing slow, deep breaths. Breathe.

Continue to release the tension from your body. Relax your arms. Relax your legs. Relax your knees. Relax your feet. Breathe. Imagine etheric cords coming out of your body, down through the floor and into the earth. See these beautiful cords of energy going down into the earth and wrapping around the Earth's core. The center. Thank the Earth for providing this environment where you can live and grow. Feel the warm and brilliant energy from the Earth. See the energy move up the cords and come into your body. Feel warm and safe. See the energy surround your whole body. Feel protected. Breathe in this beautiful energy.

Now, take a long, deep inhale through your nose. Open your mouth to let it go. Let's take two more release breaths. Inhale, all the way, through your nose. Open your mouth to release. One more. Inhale through your nose, open your mouth to release. Good.

This time, gather all the negativity from your body. See it. Give it a shape, a color, and a texture. Create it. Collect all of the negativity from all of the parts of your body. See it. Pull it out of your body and see it in a ball in front of you. Take a long, slow, deep breath in through your nose. When you exhale, open your mouth and blow away the ball of negative energy. Blow it away. Let it go. Release the negativity.

Let's do it again. Inhale through your nose. When you open your mouth to release, see the remaining negativity being blown away. Let it go. One more time. Inhale through your nose, open your mouth and blow it away. It's all gone now. See the empty space where it was and smile because it's gone. Feel lighter. Breathe normally once again.

Begin now to feel your energy. Feel it ebb and flow through and around your body. See it dance across your skin. As you inhale, draw up more energy from the cords connecting you to the earth. Feel it swirling around and mixing in with your energy. The next time you inhale again, pull the energy up from your feet, and send it all the way over your head, like a wave, or bed covers. Pull it up and put it over your head. As you exhale, push it down, down from your head, through your body, into your feet, and just beneath your feet. Feel it all around you.

Keep this pattern going, pull the energy up from your feet, over your head as you inhale, and pull it down from your head, around your feet as you exhale. Complete the circle every time you inhale and exhale. While you pull the energy up from your feet, think about bringing positive energies into your life. What kinds of positive experiences would you like to have? What does it feel like? What does it look like? Are you smiling?

Continue to inhale the energy up from your feet over your head, and exhale the energy down from your head around your feet. As you inhale the energy up, think about bringing positive people into your life. What do they look like? What do they feel like? Are they smiling? Bring them in. Keep breathing.

Imagine a large ball of brilliant white and golden energy. See it above your head. See it filled with uplifting positivity. See it come down over your head and surround your whole body with its brilliant light and positive energy. See it shielding you from negativity. See it removing obstacles out of your path. See it staying with you, always. Give it your gratitude for helping and protecting you.

Focus back on your breath. Breathing normally once again. Send thanks to the universe for helping you and giving you energy. Pull the beautiful, energetic cords up from the earth, and see them absorb back into your body. Feel whole. Feel complete. Feel safe and secure. Feel loved. Smile. If your eyes are closed, open them. See with fresh eyes. Be ready and open to new, positive energies, experiences, and people in your life. And so it is. Thank you for participating. You can find this meditation on YouTube here:

https://youtu.be/vlgZE6wrQQ0

STEP

Six

Go Within & Seek Your Answers

Step 6
Go Within & Seek Your Answers

Figure your shit out. That's what I really wanted to title this step, but "go within and seek your answers" is much prettier. Plus, that's where you will find your answers. They are already inside of you. You just need to stop and listen. If it's too scary to call it meditation, you can call it "sitting quietly."

This step is a lifelong journey in itself and does not have a quick fix. You might work through your shit, and you have it all flowing and life is beautiful, and then something comes up to knock you backward. You might think, "Oh man, I worked through this already. Why am I back here?" That's okay. It means you have to do it again. If you did it once, you could do it again.

Learn from what you did before and see if you can try a different approach this time. Dig deeper. Lessons will keep coming back until you learn what you are supposed to learn. If you want to break the cycle, you have to constantly remember to make different choices. Take the time to sleep and rest. Remember self-care! If your body is already telling you to sleep frequently, listen to it. Rest when you need to. Be easy on yourself. You can lay in bed and meditate; you don't have to be uncomfortable while meditating.

You'll have to ask yourself the hard questions. What is the baggage that you are working through? At the beginning of this guide, I talked about mine being depression. It was hard. It was hard to work through, it kept coming up, all the time, over and over, I had to clear it all away. I had to see the patterns in my decisions and behaviors, and make the choice, every time, to choose a different way. I had to face my shadow. I had to learn to love every part of myself, including the ones that I hated, the ones that I hid from myself and everyone else, and I had to learn to speak kindly to myself.

This is a great time to look into shadow work. There is so much information out there about shadow work, it's amazing and incredibly helpful. It helps you face yourself—all parts of you—and helps you learn to love everything about yourself, especially the parts that you hate. It will help you see your baggage differently. Shadow work gives you a new perspective on your anxiety, depression, physical pains and ailments, addictions, or anything else you are going through. Instead of pushing it away, embrace it, and send it love. Learn to love that part of yourself. It's hard, and it will take time and effort, but it's worth it. If you want to become a whole person, you need to complete yourself. No one else can complete you, you have to do it.

Here's a little exercise to help you with shadow work. Make a list of things that you don't like about yourself, and see how you can turn those things into positives instead of perceiving them as a negative. I'll give you an example. I used to hate the fact that I felt lazy frequently. Was I actually lazy, or was I giving my body the time it was asking for to heal? When I sat down to think about it, it was true that my body needed time for self-care. I had no idea. I just thought I was being lazy, and I was awful to myself about it. I talked negatively to myself all the time, calling myself lazy, and a loaf, and making threats to myself. I was mean!

If I talked to someone else in real life, the way I talked to myself, in my head, that person would never speak to me again. My body and soul were in great need of self-care and time to heal, but I wasn't letting it happen. I kept going, moving on to the next thing, trying to make myself happy with the next thing and the next thing, and of course, none of it was working. When I took the time to ask myself why I felt lazy and why I was being so mean, that tiny little voice inside asked me to slow down. The tiny little voice asked me for help, it asked me to slow down, and take all the time that I needed to heal. I finally sent myself love and accepted myself for the way that I am and accepted that being "lazy" was exactly what I needed to do.

Another item on my list of things that I didn't like about myself was my feet. I thought I had ugly feet. This actually was left over from childhood when other kids told me that I had ugly feet, and I believed them. Whoops. So ugly feet were on my list. To help me accept that, and own it, I used the following exercise to turn it into a positive.

I stared at my bare feet. I said, "I have ugly feet," in my head, I didn't say it out loud, but you definitely can do that, it's probably better. "I have ugly feet." Then I shifted my perspective and said, "I love my ugly feet." I asked myself, how do my ugly feet help me? My ugly feet help me walk, run, and jump every day. I said it again, "I love my ugly feet." Then I changed my perspective a little more and said, "I have beautiful feet." Again. "My feet are beautiful, they are a part of me, I am beautiful." I kept saying this every so often when I looked at my feet, "My feet are beautiful." Whenever I saw my feet. "I have beautiful feet." Eventually, I stopped thinking that my feet were ugly, and it stopped bothering me altogether.

Now, I don't think about it at all. I completely changed my perspective. I accepted my feet for what they are, accepted that they are a part of me, and changed my vocabulary. Change your vocabulary, change your perspective. Accept who you are. Learn to love and accept every part of yourself, even those things that you don't particularly care for. Ask yourself why you feel that way, ask yourself how being that way has helped you and ask yourself for acceptance. You can do it.

Once you start working through your main baggage, you can start to ask yourself about your soul's purpose. Having a direction and a goal is incredibly helpful. Something to work for and something to look forward to gives you purpose. If your goal is aligned with your soul's purpose, things will flow very naturally to you. Manifesting and setting intentions will become easy. Even if you are still working through all of your shit, if you can align yourself on the right path, life will flow. How do you do that? You start by asking yourself the tough questions.

What do you really want out of life? If you could do anything, what would it be? What do you want to do? What do you want to see? What do you want to feel? Do you want to change your life? What would it take to change your life? Don't worry about the how and all of the details right now. Let's think big picture. The universe will fill in all the details and push you in the right direction as long as your goal is aligned with your soul's purpose. Once you start asking yourself what you really want, go ahead and lay it all out there. For me, it helped to write it all down and to sit in it. (More on that in a minute.)

This is important: it is always okay to seek help from a qualified therapist or medical professional. I am not a medical professional and cannot diagnose you or prescribe medication. I can only offer helpful suggestions and share what worked for me. If your baggage is heavy and you are considering hurting yourself or others, please, put the book down and call for help. The National Suicide Prevention phone number is 1-800-273-8255.

I would like to share with you something personal about suicide. Even long after my suicidal period had passed, and I had begun healing, suicide was always there, showing its face as an option. Every time things got too hard or too overwhelming, suicide was like an old, terrible friend, showing up out of nowhere, waiving through the window, saying, *"Hey!" "Hey! I'm here! I'm always an option! Are things too hard for you? I'll make it easy! I'll take your pain away. You have never taken the easy road; life has always been hard for you. Why don't you try the easy road this time? It will be so easy, and you will find the peace that you are looking for. Let me help you."*

It was infuriating! Hearing all of that, every time things got hard, I was tired of it. It continued so far past the time that I was suicidal. This was just an old friend showing its nasty face, tempting me with "the easy way out." That's great. Except, I believe in reincarnation, and if I were to take this life, I'd probably pick a truly shitty life next time and have not only this life's shit to work through but that new life's shit to work through too, and it would suck. Or I'd come back as a honey bee, and feel so important to help pollinate food for humans and end up eating pesticides off of a dandelion and die. One of those. Anyway.

I clearly had an inappropriate relationship with suicide. What do you do when you are having an inappropriate relationship with anything? A cord cutting. I closed my eyes and tried to picture this suicide feeling/entity/thing. I gave it a face. It was a deranged-looking happy face emoji, kind of yellow, kind of grey, not quite round, hollow holes in lopsided spaces for eyes. The face looked kind of melty. Very weird and creepy.

So, I imagined this deranged suicide emoji face, and I imagined the etheric cord connecting this entity and myself. Then I pictured a giant pair of scissors. I sent the entity love and told it that I no longer needed it to be around me, it had to go, and I promised it that if it comes back, I will send it away again and cut the cord again. I saw the scissors cutting the cord. I saw the entity and that half of the cord flying away, and I sent it more love. I pulled my half of the cord back to me and sent myself love and healing. I instantly felt better, but I knew it wasn't over.

I knew I would have to do that over and over, however often that ugly suicide emoji showed its crooked face. And so I did. It became an unwanted acquaintance that I sent away and cut the cord every time. I felt so much better. Is it perfect even right now as I write these words? No. And I'm okay with that. I know that I am a work in progress, and I am giving myself time and patience as I continue to work through my own shit. One of the best things you can do for yourself is accepting where you are, for now, give yourself time and patience to heal, and then go go go!

For a longer and more thorough version of a cord cutting, you can see it on YouTube here: https://youtu.be/m37YaASzTro

Okay, back to what you really want out of life and your life path. For me, it was very helpful to write down all of my feelings and everything I was going through. I wrote about how I felt at the time, and I wrote about how I felt previously, during other hard times of my life. You can start by journaling, just write it all down. Let it flow out of your head and onto the paper or computer. Get it out of your head. What craziness are you going through? What baggage are you carrying? Write about your life. Then start to write about what you really want. Dig deep down, what do you really want? If you could do anything, what would it be? Write it down.

Another method that really worked for me was to take the time to sit in my "yuck." I would sit down and let it wash over me. I would see it, hear it, and feel it. I would allow it to have space and acknowledge its existence. You can sit with your trouble. Be with it. Allow it to come over you and accept it for what it is. Send it some love. The trick is not to stay here.

Your baggage and troubles will come up again and again until you learn the lesson that you need to learn. Don't get stuck in it. Sometimes, it can be a small thing, like a bad day or a bad moment. Allow yourself to sit in it, be with it, and give it space. Let it come over you. When you are ready, tell it that it's time to leave. You can visualize a cord cutting between you and whatever it is that you are dealing with, cut the cord, and feel the separation. Allow it to go. Once you accepted it for what it is and learned whatever you needed to learn, cut the cord and send it love, send it back into the earth to be absorbed. You don't need to carry it with you. Feel it, acknowledge it, sit with it, learn from it, and then let it go. You don't have to keep all of the baggage and the hurt and the yuck. You can let it go. I believe depression is a loss of personal power. I believe this can be applied to many other ailments in life. You have to find your power and take it back. It's important not to dwell on how you lost it, or where you lost it, (you can certainly think about it, just don't stay there) simply acknowledge that it's gone and work towards getting it back.

How do you get your power back? You have to continue to work through your baggage. It might take a long time, it will be hard. You might need help. That's okay. You're not alone. You are finding your tribe. You have your spirit guides. You have this book with resources. You can do this. Remember to ask yourself the hard questions, and then you have to be quiet enough to hear the answers.

As a stay-at-home mom, I sometimes thought my brain was going to explode from everything going on inside of it. Every once in a while, an opportunity presented itself for me to just get quiet. Every so often, my kids fell asleep in the car, and I wasn't rushing anywhere. We all sat in the parked car; they slept, and I allowed my mind to slow down and get quiet. Those quiet moments, that's where you find your answers. Monumental life answers, in a quiet moment in the car when I wasn't driving, and the kids were sleeping.

Another great place to get quiet and listen for answers is right before you fall asleep. That time after you let your mind wander, and stress and worry and plan, but before you actually fall asleep, there is a quiet moment in there. Find that moment, and let the answers come to you. Dreams are also a good place for answers. Try to remember your dreams and think about what they are telling you. When you listen to music, is there a song that really speaks to you? An easy way for your spirit guides to communicate with you is through music. You just need to be open and pay attention. You can also take time for meditation. Go back to Step 4 and find a meditation that works for you. You can meditate on a specific question. Ask the question, and wait quietly for the answer.

This will help you find your answers, work through your baggage, and take your power back. Go within and seek your answers. You already know what you want, you already know how to do it, and your power is already there, you just need to pull it out. Follow your heart. Give yourself the space and time to heal. Remember, life is a work in progress, and so are you. Be easy on yourself and have patience. Life doesn't have to be hard. You can create your own happiness.

Tip: When receiving a massage, from a massage therapist or a loved one, imagine a white or gold light coming out of their hands and fingers, going into your skin, and healing your body. You can be more specific; if you have a pulled muscle, imagine the light going deep into the muscle tissue and healing the wound. You can do this for anything, a headache, a broken bone, a bad back, arthritis, depression, anxiety, any physical or emotional pain. You can help your body heal itself.

STEP

Seven

Being An Empath Is Awesome

Step 7
Being An Empath Is Awesome

Sometimes it doesn't feel awesome. Sometimes it feels like a curse, and it feels heavy. I get it. You can literally feel the weight of the world. If there is something major going on (and when does that NOT happen?!) like rainforest fires, major destruction from earthquakes and hurricanes, war, or terrorism, you can feel the weight of the collective conscious. You can feel the trauma across the world. It's heavy. It's big. I understand. It's okay to feel it. Feel it, so you know to send it love and healing. Feel it so you can understand it, and then let it go.

Feel it, recognize it, send it love and healing, and then let it go. You can send it love and healing every day if you want to, but release it afterward. You have a beautiful gift, you can use it, and share it with the world. Just don't take it on as your own. Always remember to release it afterward. You have the power to heal yourself, to heal others, and to heal situations. You are beautiful, you are amazing, and you are special.

Not only can you walk into a room and feel what everyone is feeling, but you can make everyone feel what you are feeling. It goes both ways. You can improve the mood of the room. You can shine your light bright and improve the atmosphere. With practice, you can change the world. It's a beautiful gift.

Without thinking about it, I've been able to feel when other people use their energy to reach out to read my energy. It's pretty cool, but sometimes it's a little creepy and feels invasive. I suddenly notice that it's there. Like someone knocking on your door and looking in the windows. Are you home? Yes, I am home, thank you very much. What are you doing here? Energy exchange can be intimate. Please be cautious with whom you connect.

This includes readings, like Tarot cards, Angel cards or Runes, energy work and energy upgrades, and Psychics. It's important to know a little bit about the person you are connecting with, and it's important to trust them. After you connect energy like that, it is incredibly helpful to visualize a cord cutting. You don't want to stay connected afterward, it's like letting them stay and hang out on your front porch and stare in the windows. Send them away with love, and if you had a good experience, you could invite them back another time. When I finish a Reiki session or Rune reading, I always visualize a cord cutting. We can reconnect next time. There is no need to stay connected.

I'd like to talk to you about starseeds. What is a starseed? A starseed is someone, a soul that has come to the earth from another world or plane of existence. The starseed could be new, the soul's first life on earth, not the soul's first life, or very old and has experienced many lifetimes on earth, or somewhere in between. They are usually old souls that come here to help the people on earth transform their spiritual consciousness and go through a spiritual awakening. They help the earth move through a time of Ascension and bring positive change. Starseeds often have psychic gifts that come easily and naturally to them.

It is really important for starseeds to reconnect to their origins or home planet. Often, starseeds that come to earth feel out of place and like they don't belong. They innately know that they are not from here. Living on earth can be really hard after experiencing other parts of the cosmos. Learning the word starseed, and figuring out that I am not from here, explained so much in my life. I knew it was real because I felt it long before I understood it. Then, through a past life regression/meditation, I experienced my homeworld. Connecting to my homeworld made a huge difference in my life here. I had roots and wings. I felt more complete and more whole. It made sense, and it felt right.

It's also very important for starseeds to walk their true life path and fulfill their life's purpose. It's incredibly difficult for starseeds to have meaningless jobs and relationships. That's why I have emphasized sitting quietly and figuring out what you want from life. Figuring out what you want from life is so helpful even if you are not a starseed (by the way, it's totally fine not to be a starseed, being created on Earth is also special). Like I said in the very beginning, everyone is special, and we are all connected, no matter where we are from. We have the choice and the power to hold each other up or tear each other down.

How do you know if you are a starseed? Here are some common characteristics of starseeds:

A knowing that you are not from here

An intense feeling that you don't belong

A deep need for spirituality

You are drawn to space and the stars

You feel your life has a huge purpose, but you don't know what that is

Your life is incredibly challenging

You have medical conditions that confuse doctors

You have dreams or memories of places that are not on earth

You have psychic abilities that come easy to you

Your spiritual gifts and spiritual awakening happen fast because you have done this before

You buck the system and have trouble with authority

What do you do now? Try to connect with your homeworld, it will help you feel better. Sit with your feelings, whether they are big or small or loud or quiet, be with your feelings and accept them. Let go of what "figuring your shit out" looks like and just be with it. Follow your intuition and let it guide you through your journey.

Start to love yourself for who you are. I heard the expression, "you have to love yourself first before others can love you," but it never really sank in. I didn't understand what loving yourself meant. It means respecting yourself, setting boundaries for yourself and others. It means doing the things that you feel in your heart are right. It means following your intuition and allowing you to be you. Give yourself permission to be. Just be. Empaths have big hearts, are very generous, and genuinely care about other people and animals. You are a magical and amazing person, filled with love and warmth and care. You are special and should be treated with tender loving care from yourself and from those around you.

Sometimes, you might want to turn it off, hide it, or hide from yourself. I understand. Let me share with you. I was feeling especially sensitive for a couple of weeks and then had a bad experience at a doctor's office. I left the office in tears. When I got home, I mustered up all the courage to call them to say I wasn't paying a penny for that appointment. Later, I was more relaxed and was driving in the car. I felt compelled to send the doctor love and energy. I opened his third eye and asked him to see his behavior for what it was. I believe it worked.

I got chills and goosebumps and a great knowing that this is part of my life purpose. I started thinking about all the people I have helped in similar ways (normally it's more complicated and time consuming than sending love and opening the third eye). I have helped people find themselves, become better people, change their behavior and lives in a complete 180. Part of my life purpose is to help transform this negativity into light.

Unfortunately, that means I experience their negativity first. That sucks. When I realized that part of my purpose for being here was this transformation, I started crying (thankfully, I had arrived at my destination and was sitting in the parking lot). I was sobbing. I didn't want it. It was too hard, too much. I wanted to crawl into a hole and hibernate. I wanted a "normal" life. I didn't want to know all the things that I knew. It suddenly felt so heavy. I kept piling it on. I didn't want to see spirits, I didn't want to have spirits come to me to help them cross over, I didn't want visions of the future and past lives. I was tired of feeling everything. I didn't want to feel anymore.

So, I cried. I let it all go. I let go of my expectations of my life and my experiences. I let go of the heavy. I let it fall away. I accepted my power for what it is. I accepted myself for who I am. I am special. I have a purpose. You are special. You have a purpose. That purpose is beautiful and perfect. Accept these gifts that you have been given and see them as amazing and beautiful. You have additional information on people, places, and objects. It's like a superpower.

You can feel if someone is having a really hard time and you can be the one who is extra nice to them. It could be a cashier, someone walking down the street, someone you work with, someone that comes to your house for a service, or someone at a restaurant. You can easily be the one that makes their day better because you know how they feel without them having to tell you. (Reminder: feel their energy and then let it go; do not keep it and pile it on yourself. Boundaries!) Your power is beautiful, see it as a gift. Use it with tender loving care. You can do it. You can be the person you were meant to be. You can make your soul sing! You can be happy if you choose it. Everything is a choice. Choose love and acceptance. You are beautiful the way you are.

I love affirmations. I'm not offended if you don't. I use affirmations all the time to help stay positive, or as a pick me up, or as a good reminder for something that I need. Here are a few that I created and find useful.

Speak your truth.

Shine your light.

Be who you are.

Change your perspective, change your life.

I accept myself for who I am.

I accept others for who they are.

I accept my experiences for what they are.

It's time to let go.

It's time to cut the chains.

You can do it!

Chakra affirmation:

Root - I am grounded.

Sacral - I feel.

Solar Plexus - I am strong.

Heart - I love.

Throat - I speak my truth.

Third Eye - I see.

Crown - I am beyond.

I realize that I am already a complete person.

I am comfortable in my own skin.

I love my whole self.

I am living life fully in the present moment.

I choose joy.

These are just a few of thousands of affirmations out there. Find some that resonate with you, and say them out loud or to yourself when you need to. You can put them on sticky notes in places in front of your face (bathroom mirror, kitchen, car), you can hang them on your wall, you can save them on your phone or computer to look through when you need them. They serve as great reminders when you are feeling low or negative.

What's next?

You have finished the book! Yay! Thank you for reading it all the way through. What do you do now? Work on yourself. Continue to be open to your greatness, accept your gifts, accept your flaws (cause they aren't really flaws, they are pieces of beauty and perfection), and figure your shit out. Re-read the book if you want to, or just the section that calls to you. Practice the meditations all the time, and practice self-care as much as you possibly can. Do what you need to do. Remember, you are awesome! Being an empath is awesome. Own it, love it, and choose joy. Trust the answers that are coming from within. Follow your intuition.

I truly hope this book has given you the tools you need to transform your life and get out from under that rock that you have been carrying for however many years. You can do it. It won't be easy, but I promise it will be worth it. Is the grass greener on the other side? Plant your own green grass, water it every day, and send it love. Take care of yourself. You are in charge of your own destiny. There are additional note pages at the end of the book.

With love, light and forever gratitude,

Alicia McBride

Journal Pages

Self-care ideas: What are some things you can do to take care of yourself?

What brings me joy? Make a list of all the things that bring you joy.

Things I am grateful for:

Healing modalities I would like to try:

Additional notes:

About The Author

Alicia McBride is a creative clairvoyant empath who loves empowering people to heal themselves, writing books, and being a mom to two energetic boys. She lives in southeastern PA, enjoys dancing, digital painting, and wearing PJs in public. Alicia has a degree in Psychology and Interior Design, is a Certified Yoga Instructor, a Reiki Master, and has gone through a Spiritual Awakening (does that ever end?). Her eclectic background continues to inspire her to help others through creative outlets such as writing books and energy healing.

More Information:

HealingLightEmpath.com
Facebook.com/groups/BeginnerEmpath
YouTube.com/channel/UCPzhYbwBwZ2WTIDJdE4BRNQ
Pinterest.com/HealingLightEmpath
www.ILoveYouWhenBook.com

Made in the USA
Columbia, SC
29 March 2021